DEER
TAILS & TRAILS

DEER
TAILS & TRAILS

THE COMPLETE BOOK OF
EVERYTHING WHITETAIL

Compiled by

MICHAEL FURTMAN

WILLOW CREEK PRESS

Published by
Willow Creek Press
P.O. Box 147
Minocqua, Wisconsin 54548

Editor/Design: Andrea K. Donner

Library of Congress Cataloging-in-Publication Data:

Furtman, Michael.
Deer tails & trails : the complete book of everything whitetail / text by Michael Furtman.
    p. cm.
  ISBN 1-59543-235-3 (hardcover : alk. paper)
  1. White-tailed deer. 2. I. Title: Deer tails and trails. II. Title.
  QL737.U55F855 2006
  599.65'2--dc22

                                                            2006001124

Printed in Canada

Contents

The Story of Deer

Riveted in the edge of the forest clearing, a
tense whitetail doe swivels her ears, straining to
locate the sound that had brought her to attention.
Forty yards away her spotted fawn lays hidden beneath
a clump of brush. Flared nostrils testing the air, the doe
tightens every muscle in her body. A cry from her fawn would bring her
charging from her hiding place, ears flattened, hooves flying in defense.

No matter the size of her opponent, nor how sharp its teeth or claws, the doe would attempt to drive off any predator with a not-to-be-trifled fury. Should that fail, and there be no recourse but to flee, she would try to lead her fawn to safety. There remained the fact, however, that if neither fighting nor leading could save her fawn, she would leave it to its fate, so that she herself might live on to reproduce again.

Like whitetails of a thousand generations, she had chosen her feeding site, and the fawn's bed, with just this scenario in mind. The descendent of deer that had successfully survived just such threats, in her very molecules is an escape response to guide her. Fleet of foot, whitetail deer first try to outrun the threat. Failing that, their long, powerful legs propel them over deadfalls and brush piles, obstructions the predator must detour around, wasting valuable time. Through the impenetrable forest, they fly down well worn paths, trails that they know lead them toward safety and that harbor no surprises.

The forest, and its edge, shaped this species through its food types, bedding areas, and escape routes. The predator shaped the whitetail too, causing the evolution of senses and physical build needed to have a better-than-average chance to escape. Millions of years of natural selection led to this balance.

As the threatening noise fades into the distance, the doe relaxes her guard. Hearing no alarm from her fawn, she quietly returns to her feeding. The threat, real or imagined, had not materialized, but it was the ones that had which had shaped this species.

A Prey Species

Wherever deer live—and they live almost world-wide—it has been this predator-prey relationship that has shaped them. We see them as swift, agile athletes because they are. Being

pursued by all manner of fanged and clawed predators since before humans were human, deer have evolved to be alert, secretive and, when need be, fast afoot.

Although the roots of the white-tailed deer, the species most common in North America, fade far back into the dim mists of time, evolving from animals to which today they bear little resemblance, there was a time some 25 million years ago that their ancestors began to take on shapes we would at least recognize as some kind of grazing or browsing mammal. It was the Miocene epoch, and it was then that these plant eating mammals began to specialize. One branch began to make a living from brushy or woodland habitat, becoming browsers of leafy plants. Another branch turned to grazing, inhabiting open country with lush grasslands.

It was in the former branch, which became the *Family Cervidae*, that the white-tailed deer evolved; cows and other grazers sprung from the latter branch, called *Family Bovidae*. These families share similarities—they are all hoofed animals with multiple stomachs. And there are differences—in the family *Cervidae* antlers are grown and shed each year, while in *Bovidae* they are permanent.

"BANG!! Just kidding."

It is interesting, and explains much about the whitetails' behavior, that at such a distant time their ancestors took to the woods and its edge. The white-tailed deer that we see today have had 25 million years to perfect their way of life. For just as the deer may have itself help shape the forest, life in the forest shaped the deer both physically and behaviorally.

Leaping ahead nineteen million years, the deer of six million years ago were browsing north of the Arctic Circle, where on a very different planet Earth, lush hardwood forests then grew in the far north. We don't know exactly what these deer looked like because few fossils have survived. Later, as the climate cooled and glaciers pushed south, deer and their forests gradually retreated in advance.

The white-tailed deer evolved to live on the edges of forest habitat.

During the Pleistocene epoch, not only were ancestral white-tailed deer evolving and roaming on the North American continent, but so too were vast herds of elephants, camels, llamas, horses, and mastodons. Huge lion-like predators stalked and feasted on these mammals, and the now extinct dire wolf coursed the forests and fields, very likely testing and dining on the whitetail's ancestors. Saber-toothed cats made their living then, rending prey with sickle fangs, and giant bears roamed the earth batting to the ground with powerful forelimbs the young of even the largest mammals. Each predator specialized on a few prey, and each prey carved out its own ecological niche.

With so many other animals around, many of which were specialized in diet and habitat, the progenitor white-tailed deer did then what it does now—learned to live on the edges of forest habitat that no other browser or grazer utilized. This strategy meant that it was to flourish even as these other animals passed into extinction. The dramatic changes in climactic conditions that suddenly brought extinction to others favored the plasticity of the animal that became the white-tailed deer. It was a very different world that shaped our white-tailed deer, yet one that miraculously prepared them almost perfectly for life in today's human-dominated environment.

THE STAG-MOOSE

The stag-moose (scientific name *Cervalces scotti*) is an extinct deer slightly larger than the modern moose. Its name, stag-moose, refers to the fact that it looks much like a cross between an elk and a moose. If you had been around to see one alive, you might have thought it looked like a stilt-legged moose with the face of an elk and very complex palmate antlers. Palmate antlers are shaped like the palm of a hand, i.e. they have large flat areas and thinner projections. Modern moose (*Alces alces*) have palmate antlers; however, the stag-moose had more complex antlers than the modern moose. The stag-moose is found in deposits that indicate it probably preferred swamps, bogs, and other wetlands in environments like the tundra and spruce parklands. This habitat is similar to that preferred by modern moose. The stag-moose probably led a lifestyle very similar to that of the modern moose. Although not extremely common, specimens of the stag-moose have been found in most Midwestern states. Stag-moose went extinct between 11,000 and 10,000 years ago. (Source: Illinois State Museum)

OLD WORLD AND NEW WORLD DEER

Both Old and New World deer are also members of the larger *Family Cervidae*—animals with antlers and four-chambered ruminating stomachs that usually bear spotted young. There are 53 species in the *Family Cervidae*. The cervid's four-chambered stomach is an important adaptation, for it allowed hoofed mammals to make their way out of the tropical forests, where forage was lush, onto the grasslands and cooler northern latitudes where forage, though seasonally abundant, was often of poor quality. Grasses and woody browse are hard to digest, and the four-chambered stomach allows for fermentation, a digestive tool that uses microbacterial action to squeeze out nutrients and energy.

Whitetails and Its Near Relatives

While the white-tailed deer is certainly the most familiar species, there are actually five deer species in North America: white-tailed; moose; elk; mule deer/black-tailed deer; and caribou.

White-tailed deer are members of the genus *Odocoileus*—the genus of North American deer. Members of the genus *Odocoileus* are also found in South America, but they exist on no other continents. As members of the *Family Cervidae*, which is found worldwide, genus *Odocoileus* shares with other members these common traits: they possess antlers that are shed annually; only males grow antlers (except for caribou and reindeer); they are hoofed, and the hooves are two toed; and they have a four-chambered stomach designed for digesting woody plants.

Moose (above) and elk (right) are both deer species and members of the *Cervidae* family.

Mule deer (below) have much larger ears than whitetails, and the buck mule deer's antlers grow upward into a fork rather than sweeping forward like those of the whitetail (opposite page).

The genus *Odocoileus* includes not only the white-tail deer (*Odocoileus virginianus*), but its near relatives: the mule deer and black-tailed deer (both *Odocoileus hemionus*). There is disagreement about just exactly how these three deer species are related, but their is consensus that the whitetail is the ancestral form. Two theories exist to explain how these other deer are related to whitetails. The more traditional theory hypothesizes that the black-tailed deer erupted from the whitetail first, and that the blacktail alone gave rise to the mule deer about 10,000 years ago. More recent research into mitochondrial DNA gives rise to a new theory: that blacktails and whitetails, at some point well after they were distinct species, rejoined through hybridization, and it was these hybrids that evolved into today's mule deer. That is, a blacktail-whitetail hybrid is NOT a mule deer, but it was these hybrids that evolved into the mule deer over time.

However these deer species became distinct, the changes were both physical and behavioral. Even where they occupy the same geographic region, they are separated by their preference for food and the manner in which they avoid predators.

Mule deer differ from whitetails in a number of physical manners: they have much larger ears (hence the name), lack the whitetail's white flag-like tail, and the buck mule deer antler's main beam grows upward into a fork rather than sweeping forward like that of the whitetail. The black-tailed deer bears some resemblance to the whitetail, from which it presumably sprang. Although its antlers also fork similarly to the mule deer's, the effect is not as pronounced. In fact, the antlers of some blacktail subspecies, such as the Sitka deer, sweep forward much like that of the whitetail.

Both blacktails and mule deer have a whitish rump patch, but that of the mule deer is larger. The tail of both is narrower than the broad brush of the whitetail's. As per its name, the tail of the blacktail is dark down its outer surface's length. The mule deer's tail is whitish, but tipped in dark hair. Where the bridge of a white-tailed deer's muzzle is dark gray or brown, that of the mule deer is creamy white. The black-tailed deer again splits the difference in coloration, containing patches of both colors.

The whitetail deer's antlers sweep forward into a basket shape.

Behavioral difference evolved from each deer's preference of habitat—or habitat differences evolved from each form's behavioral differences.

Let me explain. The choice of food for each form is remarkably similar, which would lead one to believe that they could easily move into each other's territory. Instead, differences in behavior seem to be the key that separate the three; the most dramatic difference is their respective strategies for evading predators.

Given a choice, all three deer prefer to hide from predators. But when that fails, each has its own escape routine. Whitetails choose to run at high speed from danger. They are built for swiftness and quick maneuvering. Intimately familiar with their home territory, white-tailed deer use familiar trails when threatened because they can speed down them knowing that they do not lead to dead-ends or into obstructions. Thus the forest is an aid in their escape, not a hindrance.

Whitetails (opposite page) are built for swiftness and quick maneuvering, while mule deer (below) are masters at evading predators in the rough terrain of the west.

Like their whitetail cousins, mule deer are masters at hiding in relatively sparse cover. With its large ears to sense far off trouble, it often chooses to remain motionless in the hope of escaping detection or to sneak quietly from the scene. But when trouble can't be avoided, the mule deer also runs from danger. How it flees, however, is very different than that of the whitetail. Instead of running down forest trails, mule deer seek out obstacles or rough terrain. In such broken cover they can quickly switch directions or bound over boulders, trees, and other obstacles that predators must avoid. Mule deer are able to do this largely because of their gate—known as a "stott"—which is a peculiar bounding form of running. Using this pogo stick technique, they frequently flee uphill, for their powerful bounds and precise foot placement in broken terrain give them even further advantage over predators. Thus, although it could biologically survive on the same diet of the forest whitetail, its escape strategy has evolved for the open, often arid country of the West.

Mule deer (above and left), and a black-tailed deer (opposite page).

Of the three types of deer, the black-tailed deer is perhaps the master of hiding. Often hiding for most of the day in the dense forest of the precipitous Pacific Coast, its home range, blacktails favor feeding at night. Because the forest is so dense, they often hear a predator before the predator senses them. If they can escape by hiding motionless, they will, but when forced to flee they stott much like a mule deer, the rough topography dictating that this form of running is more effective than the whitetail's hell-bent-for-leather dash.

Hybridization does occur between the species where their ranges overlap, particularly between whitetails and mule deer. These hybrids are neither "fish nor fowl" so to speak. Because they have inherited neither species' escape strategy intact, they frequently act confused when approached by prey, and are poorly suited for long-term survival. Differences in breeding habits, particularly in the manner in which bucks of the species court or pursue does and contest among themselves, keeps hybridization to a minimum.

AFTER EUROPEAN SETTLEMENT

White-tailed deer flourished on the North American continent before the coming of humans, but the presence of Native people didn't adversely impact the species much. The real changes came after European settlement.

What we think of as the vast, unbroken forests of pre-European America were in fact not unbroken at all. Natural

events such as forest fires, tornadoes, diseases, hurricanes, and insects caused repeated eruptions of new forest growth, the type of growth that favors white-tailed deer. In addition, even mature forests that provide mast crops, such as acorns, proved suitable for whitetails. Native people also altered the landscape, frequently using fire to their own advantage to burn back forests to provide openings for berry production, for safety near regularly used seasonal encampments, and for agriculture. So although today's landscape, with its widespread conversion to agriculture and frequent forest cropping in many ways has benefited white-tailed deer, the forest primeval was in no way inhospitable to this remarkable animal.

There is some disagreement among researchers as to whether or not whitetail numbers were historically higher than today. A commonly held view is that the white-tailed deer is a prime example of the effectiveness of modern wildlife management. To a degree, this is true, for in many areas the whitetail was driven to near extinction. Scientific wildlife management was critical to returning whitetails to abundance.

However, to assume that the historical, pre-European whitetail numbers were lower than today is possibly erroneous, for the steep decline of whitetails was due primarily to overharvesting by market gunners trading in venison and hides, the subsistence use of white-tailed deer as food by settlers, and to temporary changes in habitat as the westward expansion progressed.

An analysis of available historical data, combined with American Indian population figures, archeological evidence of these peoples' diet, and reports from the earliest settlers chronicling whitetail encounters and abundance, seems to indicate that white-tailed deer were at least as abundant during pre-European times as they are today.

The whitetail deer was very important to American Indians, and in many cases, the meat of whitetails was the single largest contributor to their animal protein consumption. Examinations of bones found in middens (essentially, ancient garbage dumps) reveal that the diets of even those tribes that were agricultural or fisher-folk depended heavily upon white-tailed deer. Using formulas based on the amount of bones found at these sites and population estimates of American Indians in whitetail range, the two McCabes calculated that Indian harvest of whitetails ranged between 4.6 and 6.4 million deer annually, and that in order for this harvest to be sustainable over long periods, white-tailed deer must have numbered some 23-33 million strong.

*"I don't even care if I get a deer.
I'm just going for the solitude."*

Ernest Thompson Seton (1860-1946), early American naturalist, author and artist, once calculated that, based on his own travels and records and those of numerous early European explorers, the white-tail deer inhabited about three million square miles in the United States and Canada in pre-settlement times. This range, questioned by some researchers yet upheld by others, is virtually identical to today's whitetail range, with the possible exception of some parts of Canada, and perhaps northeastern Minnesota, where logging has most definitely helped the whitetail expand northward to replace the native woodland caribou.

WHITETAIL SUBSPECIES AND RANGE

The white-tailed deer's range stretches from beyond the 60th parallel in Canada, near the Arctic Circle, south across the straits of Panama into South America to 18 degrees south latitude in Peru. In various densities, they occupy country from the Atlantic coast westward into Washington state and Oregon. A line drawn diagonally from the southwestern corner of Washington to Texas marks the major boundary between whitetails (to the east) and mule deer/blacktails (to the west). However, this boundary is not absolute. Some populations of whitetails exist in pockets to its west, and mule deer live in some niches to its east.

Whitetails can be found in 48 states—only Hawaii and Alaska are lacking whitetails. However, whitetails are very rare in some western states such as Nevada and Utah. In Canada, whitetails can be found in Alberta, Saskatchewan, Manitoba, Ontario, Quebec, and New Brunswick. About 25 million white-tailed deer live in this U.S.-Canadian range.

Mule deer are named for their large, nine-inch long, mule-like ears.

Where their ranges overlap, mule deer inhabit the open country and hilly uplands, while whitetails prefer the bottomland forests along rivers. The Coues subspecies of whitetail is an exception, and lives in arid portions of Arizona and New Mexico, and Texas whitetails inhabit brushy, but otherwise open, plains. The range of the white-tailed deer seems to be encroaching on that of the mule deer, most probably due to habitat changes resulting from agriculture that favors the whitetail.

In the United States and Canada, there is, in general, about a two month difference in the dates of important whitetail events, north to south. That is, whitetails in northern Minnesota enter the breeding season, develop antlers, and give birth about two months earlier than those in Texas. Events for these northern deer must take place in a more constricted time period in order to insure that fawns are born at the most hospitable time (after the last winter storms) but early enough to allow for maximum growth before the return of winter. With less critical constraints placed upon them, the timing of these events in southern subspecies exhibit a wider range of dates. For instance, northern whitetail bucks in a particular area may come into rut virtually simultaneously, while the rut of their southern brethren will take place over a longer period of time.

Wherever whitetails are found, their habitat preferences are similar, although they may appear different to our eyes. Thick cover is preferred for hiding and fawning, and is a component of all whitetail's home territory. While that may consist of dense young forest in Michigan, in the arid southwest, thick stands of cactus or dense brush may serve the same purpose. Similarly, forest openings, which serve as places where white-tailed deer can gather and socialize, or where bucks can display and spar, are important to whitetails throughout their range, though the cause and appearance of these openings differs from Montana to Florida. Optimal whitetail range provides diversity; in addition to both forest openings and thick areas, food resources are varied, containing trees, lush forbs, grasses, shrubs, and weeds.

SUBSPECIES CLASSIFICATION

The Carmen Mountains subspecies is the second-smallest deer. The Key deer subspecies (opposite page) is the smallest deer, standing about 28" at the shoulder.

In total, their are 38 subspecies of white-tailed deer recognized across its entire range; thirty in North and Central America and eight in South America. In the United States and Canada, science currently recognizes seventeen subspecies of Odocoileus virginianus. Several of these subgroups are rare or endangered, such as the Columbian whitetail that survives only on a refuge near Washington's Columbia River, and the island-bound Florida Key deer. Others exist in isolation: there are four tiny populations located on islands off the Atlantic Coast of Georgia and South Carolina. The Mexican subspecies known as the Carmen Mountains whitetail just barely ranges into America.

All whitetails are classified as *Odocoileus virginianus*. First recognized as *Odocoileus virginianus virginianus* in 1780, all other subspecies have been given the *Odocoileus virginianus* name, with the subspecies name following. In the above example the Virginia whitetail is classified as *O.v. virginianus*. Others are similarly abbreviated: the Northern Woodland whitetail is *O.v. borealis*. The subspecies found in the United States and Canada are listed on the next page.

SUBSPECIES	LOCATION
Columbian whitetail – O.v. leucurus	Eastern WA & OR
Northwest whitetail – O.v. ochrourus	Western WA & OR; northern CA; southern British Columbia; ID; western MT & WY; northern UT
Dakota whitetail – O.v. dacotensis	Southern Alberta, Saskatchewan, Manitoba; eastern MT & WY; ND; SD; NE; northern CO.
Northern Woodland whitetail – O.v. borealis	MN; WI; MI; IL; IN; OH; PA; MD; DE; CN; RI; NY; MA; VT; NH; ME; New Brunswick; Nova Scotia; southern Quebec & Ontario
Virginia whitetail – O.v. virginianus	VA; WV; KY; TN; NC; SC; GA; AL; MS
Bull's Island whitetail – O.v. taurinsulae	SC
Hunting Island whitetail – O.v.venatorius	SC
Hilton Head whitetail – O.v. hiltonensis	SC
Blackbeard Island whitetail – O.v. nigribarbis	SC
Florida whitetail – O.v. seminolus	Southern GA; most of FL
Florida Key whitetail – O.v. clavium	Florida Keys islands
Florida coastal whitetail – O.v. osceola	FL panhandle, southwest coastal AL; coastal MS
Kansas whitetail – O.v. macrourus	IA; MO; AR; northern LA; northeast TX; eastern OK & KS; southeastern NE
Avery Island whitetail – O.v. mcilhennyi	coastal TX & LA
Texas whitetail – O.v. texanus	Western TX, OK & KS; southeastern CO; eastern NM
Carmen Mountains whitetail – O.v. carminsis	TX (near Big Bend)
Coues whitetail – O.v. couesi	Southern half AZ; southwest NM

Key deer

The Virginia, Northern Woodland, Dakota, and Texas whitetail subspecies enjoy both the largest ranges and greatest numbers. In most states only one subspecies is found, although where ranges meet, the distinction between subspecies becomes vague. Some experts put the Texas whitetail's range as far north as southern South Dakota; others believe its range ends in northern Kansas. Similarly, the Dakota whitetail probably overlaps onto the plains of western Minnesota, and it is possible that the Kansas whitetail may range north of the Iowa border into Minnesota.

Except for variations in body and antler size, and differences in coat color, the white-tailed deer is remarkably similar throughout its range. That doesn't mean there aren't differences. Body size of northern subspecies is always larger than those in the south, often considerably. And northern deer tend to be darker of coat as well. The differences are greater as the distance between subspecies increases.

The tiny Key deer (left) is endangered, with only about 800 deer left today. They mainly live in a six-mile area with most of the population on Big Pine Key (Florida).

Just how much bigger are northern white-tailed deer? The largest deer seem to come from the Northern Woodland (boreal) whitetail subspecies. Live weight whitetails of 300 pounds are taken with fair regularity in Minnesota, also the state where the largest whitetail ever recorded was killed in 1926: a giant of 511 pounds, undressed. Measured average weights of bucks of the subspecies clearly reflect Bergmann's Rule (keep in mind that does weigh about 60 percent of bucks of the same age):

SUBSPECIES	Average Weight (bucks)
Northern Woodlands (boreal) whitetail	240 pounds
Dakota whitetail	225 pounds
Northwest whitetail	225 pounds
Kansas whitetail	200 pounds
Virginia whitetail	175 pounds
Texas whitetail	150 pounds
Florida whitetail	150 pounds
Florida coastal whitetail	140 pounds
Carmen Mountains whitetail	120 pounds
Coues whitetail	100 pounds
Key whitetail	80 pounds

Nothing in nature, however, is quite that easily plotted. Variations occur even within the range of a single subspecies since nutrition plays a huge role in physical development.

BERGMANN'S RULE

The tendency for northerly members of a species to be larger than southern relatives is known as Bergmann's Rule. In essence, large bodies more efficiently retain body heat because the ratio of internal volume to external surface area is an improvement over that of smaller members of the species. They simply lose heat at a slower rate. Northern whitetail's darker coats may also be thermally related: the darker a surface, the more solar energy it absorbs. Of course, a dark coat in a northern coniferous forest probably is better camouflage; lighter-colored coats in the plains states are then logical. In the tropics of South America, the whitetail's red summer coat is worn year round. At mountain elevations in Peru, the winter coat passes for daily wear throughout the year. The ears of northern whitetails are generally smaller than those in warmer climes, which serves to avoid frostbite in northern deer, while the larger ears of those in the south probably radiate heat more efficiently, helping to keep them cooler.

MOOSE

Few might think of the Moose (*Alces alces*) as a deer, but there you have it. The moose (known as Elk in Europe—I know, it's confusing!) is our largest deer. Once more common than it is today, it still has a very large range, from the forests of the Northeast, populations in some Great Lakes states (mostly the Upper Peninsula of Michigan and northern Minnesota) to the uplands of North Dakota and into the Rocky Mountains. By far the largest populations exist across Canada, nearly from coast to coast, and well north into Alaska.

Moose are found circum-polar, which just means that wherever coniferous forests are found, whether in northern Europe, northern Asia, or North America, there are moose. At over seven feet in height and growing up to 1,500 pounds, the moose is as large as a horse, and it is the largest deer in the world.

MOOSE TRIVIA

• The sound of the bull is a tremendous bellow; however, it also croaks and barks during the mating season.

• Moose can run 35 mph for short distances, and can easily swim 10 miles without stopping.

• The points on the antlers of a moose may grow as much as a centimeter a day during the month of June.

• The record antler spread for a bull moose is 6 feet 9 inches.

• Newborn calfs weigh 24 to 35 pounds.

• A moose can store more than 100 pounds of food in its stomach.

• Moose can live up to 20 years.

• Moose have weak eyesight and have actually mistaken cars for potential mates.

• According to a Google search result, it's illegal to feed alcoholic beverages to moose in Fairbanks, Alaska.

Like other deer, moose are herbivores, and favor willow, aspen, and other succulent trees as food. It is thought that the word "moose" derives from the Algonquian Indian word "mooswa," which means "animal that strips bark from trees."

Moose have heavy hides and coats, well suited to northern environments. In warm weather, they enjoy wallowing in mud. In summer, they shed their heavy coat, and also

switch to eating aquatic plants, and so are common along lazy streams, lily-pad lined lake shores, and in marshes and beaver ponds. With long, thin legs, they negotiate rough country with surprising ease. Both males and females have a fleshy flap beneath their throat called a bell, but only males have antlers—which can grow to six feet across! The antlers are shed around November or December, after mating season has ended.

Woodsman consider the moose the most dangerous animal in the forest. Why? During mating season, bull moose are truly belligerent, and have been known to charge people, cars, and even trains!

Today, the moose is our largest deer and carries the largest antlers (over six feet across), but around 5,700 BC, the now-extinct Irish Elk (*Megaloceros giganteus*) roamed Europe and Ireland. It is famous for its formidable size (about two meters at the shoulder), and for having the largest antlers of any known *cervid*—a maximum of 13 feet from tip to tip! A significant collection of Irish Elk skeletons are held at the Natural History branch of the National Museum of Ireland, Dublin.

ELK – OR WAPITI

When the first Europeans came to North America, they called the large deer they saw "elk" applying the name they used in Europe for what we call moose. But elk and moose are two very different critters, and our elk already had many names given to them by the native peoples, the most commonly known of which is Wapiti.

The last elk killed in Pennsylvania, and perhaps the last native elk killed anywhere in the east, met its lonely demise in November 1867. It might come as a surprise to many that elk

were once found in almost every state and province in the U.S. and Canada. Their range at the time of European settlement may have exceeded that of the white-tailed deer, the latter often considered to be this continent's most adaptable deer. Perhaps we should have saved that title for the elk, the most highly evolved and adaptable of the Old World deer.

The early natural history text, *Lives of Game Animals* by Earnest Thompson Seaton, quotes a 1806 journal article written by Dr. B.S. Barton as follows: "Within the memory of many persons now living, the droves of Elks which used to frequent the salines west of the river Susquehanna in Pennsylvania, were so great that for 5 or 6 miles leading to the 'licks,' the paths of these animals were as large as many of the great public roads of our country. Eighty Elks have sometimes been seen in one herd upon their march to the salines."

Eventually the elk became an item of commerce, slaughtered in numbers by white market hunters (and assisted by some Indians). These gunners commonly took only the hide (which in the 1870s was worth $7.00 compared to $4.00 for a bison's), tongue and tusks, leaving the rest to rot. Although the slaughter of elk was less visible than that of the bison, it was nearly as complete. By 1881, when almost all bison were eradicated, there were still some 5,000 hide hunters scouring the West, searching out elk. It is remarkable, really, that any elk survived. By 1907, it is estimated that only 41,000 elk survived, down from a number that certainly was in the millions. Today, thanks to sound conservation, about one million elk again roam.

ELK TRIVIA

- Elk are large animals with conspicuous ears and a small (5.8" long) beige tail.

- Bulls weigh 600-1,090 pounds, averaging 700 pounds. They are about 25% larger than cows.

- Cows weigh 450-650 pounds.

- Newborn calves weigh 20-45 pounds.

- Elk live an average of 18-22 years.

- A bull's bugle begins with a low, stirring, clear note and rises to a loud, high-pitched, shrill whistle or scream, and ends with a series of short grunts. Only the whistle echoes and is heard over long distances. Bull bugling is heard during breeding season, especially in the evening.

MULE DEER AND BLACK-TAILED DEER

Much the same size as the white-tailed deer, the mule deer is found only in the west of the North American continent. In fact, this deer evolved here and has no near relatives in the Old World. Mule deer live throughout western North America from the southern Yukon to northern Mexico.

An animal of open plains and brushy hill country, the range of the mule deer overlaps that of whitetails. For instance, in Montana you might find whitetails in the bottom lands along a river, and find mule deer very nearby on the rising foothills. Because their ranges overlap, and because they are fairly similar species, mule deer and whitetails have been known to interbreed, although their offspring are unable to reproduce.

The mule deer gets its name from its large mule-like ears, which usually are about one-quarter larger than those of the white-tailed deer. "Mulies"—as they are known—have an obvious white rump patch and a small, rope-like white tail with a black tip.

The black-tailed deer is considered a subspecies of the mule deer and does interbreed with the mule deer. It is largely a deer of the Pacific rim, and ranges from California well north into Alaska.

CARIBOU

Historically, caribou were found in all northern latitudes, but are now extinct in many parts of their range. The largest herds now occur in arctic tundra regions of Alaska, Canada, Scandinavia, and Russia. In all but North America, they are called reindeer, and have been domesticated in many places where they are herded much like others herd sheep. In North America, they were once found south into Minnesota and Maine.

Currently, there are 30 herds in North America. Some, in Washington and Idaho, number less than 30 animals. The seven largest herds fluctuate between 50,000 and 200,000 animals. The largest herds tend to be barren ground caribou that live in tundra environments. The woodland caribou, which is slightly smaller, is the native caribou of the Rocky Mountains and eastern Canada, and was the species found in Minnesota and Maine.

CARIBOU TRIVIA

- The caribou's most important adaptation to winter is its ability to smell lichens beneath the snow.

- All the calves in a herd are born over a span of 5 days.

- Caribou are the only member of the deer family in which both sexes grow antlers.

- Caribou live an average of 8 to 10 years.

- The Laplanders herd the caribou for the tender caribou meat and warm hide. The hide is often used for blankets, clothing, and shelter. They use the antlers and bones for toys, tools, and weapons.

Caribou are larger than whitetails, but smaller than elk—a big bull caribou might weigh nearly 400 pounds. Unlike all of our other deer, where only males sport antlers, both male and female caribou grow new antlers each year. The male's, however, are considerably larger.

Whitetails Impact on Moose & Caribou

White-tailed deer are hosts to a meningeal worm, *P. tenuis*. Although harmless to whitetails, *P. tenuis* is often fatal to moose and caribou. It is speculated that as logging modified habitats to make them favorable to whitetails, deer moving north carried this disease into the southern ranges of moose and caribou, resulting in the latter two species' disappearance.

What is a Reindeer?

Reindeer (*Rangifer tarandus*) are semi-domesticated caribou. Although similar, there are fundamental differences between reindeer and their wild cousins, caribou. Reindeer are shorter and stouter. Reindeer bulls are smaller than caribou bulls, but cows may weigh the same as caribou cows. Coloration differences may be too subtle to notice between many reindeer and caribou; however, reindeer tend to be lighter

Reindeer are shorter and stouter than wild caribou.

with occasional pinto or white haircoats. The nose bridge, or face, of reindeer are flatter than caribou. Reindeer tend to stay in more cohesive groups. When herded or chased they tend to run in a tight group, whereas caribou often scatter. These traits are the result of domestication. It is believed they have been domesticated in Eurasia for at least 7,000 years, which is longer than the horse. In Eurasia, reindeer are classified as either domesticated or wild. Only in North America are "wild reindeer" called caribou.

The Deer—
Inside and Out

Four stomachs—it's what it takes!
So how does a stomach influence a species?
Consider this: if a deer must stand long enough in
one spot to thoroughly chew its food until it is digestible,
the deer is also exposing itself to predators for long periods
of time, which isn't a good idea! The whitetail's digestive system
accounts for a great deal of its success as a species.

Fruit trees are a favorite of whitetails.

The whitetail's compound stomach is comprised of four chambers: the rumen, reticulum, omasum, and abomasum. Cud chewing and a four-part stomach may not sound like particularly exciting topics for discussion, but the system is remarkable and helps the whitetail thrive. Unless you are a herd animal, which the whitetail is not, and enjoy the safety of the herd's many eyes and ears, standing around for long periods of time exposed to predators, isn't a sound strategy. The solitary, secretive white-tailed deer's evolutionary path selected a process that avoided such exposure to predators. By being able to digest and chew food at a later time, a deer can browse and move, making it a more difficult target to find. When it has consumed a sufficient quantity of food, it travels to a secure hiding area, brings the food back up, and chews its cud in relative leisure and safety.

Picky Eaters?

White-tailed deer (as well as black-tailed and mule deer), unlike some other deer species elsewhere in the world, utilize a selective feeding technique called "concentrate selecting." In essence, this means that they selectively choose more digestible plants, or the most digestible parts of plants, rather than consuming large quantities of less digestible food. They rarely stand around in one place for long, but prefer to nip and move. Selecting the most nutritious plant parts allows them to minimize the amount of time actually spent feeding and, thus, the amount of time they are susceptible to predators.

"Now we know where they're feeding."

The fact that deer can be choosy means they have a slightly different digestive system than other ruminants. The whitetails' rumen is smaller than that of other deer, and their salivary glands are larger.

Once they've temporarily eaten their fill and stored the food in the rumen (the stomach's first chamber), white-tailed deer move to an area in their territory they consider safe. Here they bed down, and once they are confident that no danger awaits them, they regurgitate a ball, or bolus, of food. Also known as a "cud," this partially digested food is moved into the back of their mouth for further chewing, where it is ground between their molars.

Cud chewing allows whitetails to mechanically break down fibrous foods. Saliva begins the chemical digestion, and once the plant material is ground into small particles, it passes back down the esophagus to the rumen. A cud may contain not only the plant matter the deer had only recently browsed, but also partially digested food from an earlier feeding. Food may stay in a whitetail's stomach anywhere from just hours to a few days, depending on its digestibility. Thus, in relative safety, the deer can "eat" without moving, all the while keeping alert for danger, thanks to the evolutionary advantage of their four-chambered stomach and the lowly, unexciting cud.

During most of the year, and throughout most of its geographic range, white-tailed deer can choose from a variety of succulent plants. Their diet changes with the seasons and with their physiological requirements, and those needs are different for deer of different ages or sex. For instance, does are severely stressed just before they wean their nursing fawns in early autumn, but bucks are at their nutritional peak, having spent the summer building reserves for what is their biggest challenge—the rut. Mature bucks weigh thirty percent more than same-age females, but have a lower metabolic rate. This seems to allow them to subsist on poorer fair than does; the does' dependency on more nutritious foods is likely related to the energy requirements of pregnancy and nursing.

DAILY ROUTINE

One would think that by being predictable a prey species might leave itself vulnerable to a predator smart enough to figure out the routine. The whitetail's success as a species, however, seems to indicate that an orderly routine is more of a survival advantage than a disadvantage.

Whitetails spend their day (and most of their life) doing three things: browsing, ruminating, and resting. During all of these activities they maintain a near constant vigilance, rarely sleeping for more than a few minutes at a time. In order to do these things successfully, a whitetail's home range contains two feeding areas—one for daylight, one for nighttime—and a secure bedding area.

Whitetails in the Southwest frequently consume prickly pear cactus during the summer, while their cousins in the Southeast eat grapes, and Midwestern whitetails eat late varieties of berries. Fruits are a much favored food of whitetails wherever they live. The variety they'll eat is only limited by the location and season—apples, blueberries, persimmons, blackberries, and huckleberries among the most desirable. Obviously, whitetails in more southerly latitudes enjoy an advantage in this regard, since warmer weather and longer growing seasons provide more of a bounty.

But it is the succulent parts of woody plants that are the most important component of the whitetail's diet. Leafy portions of trees and shrubs, such as red-osier dogwood, aspen, oak, and an array of vines, find their way frequently to the whitetail's menu. In some areas, agricultural plants are an important source of nutrition, and they eat not only the ripened plant, but the seeds and fresh shoots.

You can lead a deer to water... but you can't make it drink. In fact, it may not even need to drink. Although whitetails will drink large amounts of water during hot weather, most of their water needs are met by the food they consume. In general, the amount of water they drink is inversely proportional to the amount of water in their food. In the winter, they sometimes eat snow to get the water they need.

LIGHT SLEEPERS

Whitetails remain bedded for less than two hours at a time, and even during this period, they are usually awake chewing their cud (ruminating) or grooming themselves. For short periods of time, they may tuck their head into their flanks, or rest it on their haunch, and go to sleep. These sleep periods last only a few minutes at a time.

Deer beds tend to be nearer food at night, and in dense cover at higher elevation during the day. In the winter, beds are chosen for protection from wind and snow, and to be in the sun, for solar warming.

HOME RANGE

For most of its life, the average white-tailed deer will live in an area of about one square mile. This area is often called its "home range" and the final size and shape of it will depend on where its resources are located. In its home range a deer will find all its basic needs—hiding cover, food, and water—through most of the year.

WHITETAIL HOME RANGE

• Home ranges are usually oval in shape.

• Fidelity to a home range is so strong that deer have been known to starve to death because they wouldn't migrate to food only a short distance away.

• Bucks wander more than does, and so have larger home ranges.

• Some whitetails, many mule deer, and most elk are migratory—they move from a summer range to a winter range.

• Southern deer tend to be much less migratory than northern deer.

GLANDS—THEY'RE MORE THAN JUST SMELLY

Glands—those mysterious chemical producing organs found in the oddest of locations—exert tremendous control over the seasonal routine of the whitetail.

Deer possess two types of glands: sebaceous and suboriferous. Both types of glands are located just beneath the skin surface, and, in addition to their communication role, serve to weatherproof skin and hair. Sebaceous glands are often found near the base of a hair follicle where they produce an oily material called fatty lipids. These lipids aren't the source of the pheromones we're talking about, but they do contribute to the transmission of these odors which are manufactured elsewhere; the lipids transport the pheromones to tufts of hair where they are suspended, exposed, and released.

This mature buck (below) is licking his tarsal gland, while the dominate buck (opposite page) is licking the forehead scent gland of another buck.

Glands that are either known to have, or are suspected to have, some role in communication are located on the whitetails' forehead, in its nose, near its eyes, between its toes, on two locations on its rear legs, near its tail, and near the buck's penis. The roles of some glands aren't fully understood, especially those near the tail (caudal glands), penis (preputial glands), and nose (nasal gland), which have only recently been discovered.

"Not tonight, deer."

Two of the most important glands seem to be the preorbital and tarsal glands. Found just in front of the eye, the preorbital gland is a hairless, shallow slit-like pocket. Witnessing a deer scent mark a twig with this gland brings on an involuntary twinge in the human observer, for it almost appears that the deer is poking a stick into its eye. Bucks frequently rub the preorbital gland on twigs that overhang buck scrapes. Researchers don't know what message is conveyed by the scent emitted from this gland, but it certainly is of importance to whitetails, for passing whitetails definitely stop to check the odor left at these sites. Not only do rutting bucks frequently use this gland on overhead twigs, they flare it during displays of dominance, as do does when they are nursing their fawns.

The buck in the top image is using his preorbital gland at a scrape.

The tarsal gland is located on the inside of the whitetail's leg at the tarsal joint. It is marked by a raised tuft of long hairs that cover a large quantity of both sebaceous and sudoriferous glands. Like a large brush, this tuft becomes "painted" with the pheromones released from within, as well as with urine, which the deer deposits on this gland through a behavior called "rub urination." Also called "scent urination," in this technique deer of both sexes hunch up slightly and urinate on the inside of their rear legs.

Many chemical clues about a deer's fitness, readiness to breed, and perhaps even dominance, are carried in its urine, and the tarsal gland provides a means of broadcasting those clues. Special muscles under the skin, called "arrector pili" allow the whitetail to flair this gland to discharge a spurt of scent. As the breeding season progresses, the tarsal gland of mature bucks becomes stained from the frequent rub urination, and the odor of it is detectable even by humans. The tarsal gland is generally considered to be the most important of the "communication" glands.

This buck is demonstrating "scent urination," in which he hunches and urinates on the inside of his rear legs.

A newly-born fawn's footprint compared to the size of a dime.

WHERE THE RUBBER MEETS THE ROAD

Speed and stealth for the whitetail begins "where the rubber meets the road"—or in their case, where the keratin meets the detritus (OK—in lay terms, where the outer hoof meets the earth).

The whitetail's narrow, tapered hooves are specialized to allow minimal contact with the ground. This serves them well in two ways: minimal contact reduces friction, which increases speed; and narrow hooves are easier to place quietly amidst the forest floor's noisy leaves and sticks. In addition, whitetails are "perfect walkers," which simply means that while walking at normal speed, the rear hooves fall exactly into the tracks of the front hooves. The advantage of this seems fairly obvious: once the front hooves have been safely and quietly placed, the deer knows that its rear steps will be equally well-placed.

The track of a whitetail hoof is like that of paired commas, the two halves clearly revealing that they are cloven hoofed creatures, which puts them, along with sheep, goats and cows, in the order *Artiodactyla*—the order of even-toed ungulates.

Whitetails have been clocked at 36 miles per hour at full gallop. From a dead stop, whitetails can clear a fence or windfall of up to seven feet; once running, that vertical height increases to over eight feet.

If you thought that the whitetail's hooves are feet, guess again. They are really toes, the entire lower leg from the first joint or "knee" actually being an elongated foot. The hoof itself is comprised of the outer, tough horn made of keratin (our fingernails are made of the same material), and a spongy surface on the sole that provide some shock absorption and traction. Deer hooves wear constantly, and like our own nails, are replaced as they wear, although the rate of growth varies with the season. Hooves grow slowest in the winter and fastest in late summer and early autumn. Deer living where soil is very soft can develop over-grown hooves because of insufficient wear. In general, though, whitetail hoof growth matches wear pretty perfectly—about two and a half inches per year.

MORE TOES THAN YOU THINK

Looking at a whitetail's tracks, one would easily assume that they only have two toes per leg. If you guessed that, you'd be exactly half right, since there are two other vestigial toes further up the back of the leg, known as dew claws. Dew claws correspond to our pointer and pinkie fingers while the two halves of the hoof compare to our middle and ring fingers. The front leg's dew claws are nearer to the hoof than those of the rear. Usually dew claws don't show in tracks unless the deer has been walking in snow or mud, or running at high speed.

DEAR DEER HEARING

You and I have eyesight that perceives depth of field, or distance. Our hearing, however, does not, built as we are with immobile ears set on either side of our head. The whitetail's ears, however, sit atop the head, and can move independently of each other. It isn't uncommon to see a deer with one of these large "audible scoops" facing one direction, with the other pointing off somewhere else. They may even keep one ear forward and another rearward while at full gallop, so that they might hear if they're being pursued from behind, while they simultaneously listen for trouble ahead. By being able to direct its ears, whitetails not only hear better than us, it permits them to determine the direction and distance from which a sound emanates by comparing the time it takes the sound to reach the ears. If it reaches the left ear first, then whatever made the sound is nearer to that side, and through comparing the minute difference in time it takes the sound to reach each ear, they can effectively triangulate to get a fix on the source.

"It's either two big does and a buck, three small bucks, three big does, a doe with two big fawns, or three of the damndest fawns I've ever seen."

While humans tend to turn toward a sound, deer may just turn an ear toward it. By doing so, the noise is amplified. For gathering sound waves, whitetails have four times the ear surface area than do humans. In addition, they can hear sounds that we can't, particularly at the higher frequencies. White-tailed deer can hear sounds in the 500 to 12,000 Hertz range (humans hear from 20 to 20,000 Hz). The deer's hearing isn't supreme in the animal world, though. Dogs can hear better, being able to discern sounds in a range that begins lower (15 Hz) and ends higher (44,000 Hz).

The Nose Knows

When it comes to warning deer of danger, the sense of smell is the ultimate judge. Hearing a noise, the deer will look in that direction. Seeing what is making that noise may cause the deer to stare intently, but even when taken together, the deer still may not be able to identify the intruder, or be inclined to flee. One good whiff, however, is enough to finally pass judgment. And of course, a deer needn't see a human, wolf, or cougar to know that it needs to disappear. Seeing a predator simply isn't required when you can smell it.

Scent is also an important communication tool, especially for fawns and does trying to keep track of each other, as a means of finding a prospective mate, and for detecting invisible, chemical sign-posts that tell bucks about each other's rank and territory. Deer can scent track each other, a useful tool in following other deer to safety, food, or for mating.

Buck Snorts

Hunters describe the explosive sound of a deer that has scented a human a "buck snort," but actually, this call isn't limited to bucks. This common sound is made by bucks and does alike and is caused by the sudden expelling of air through the nasal passage. It serves as a warning to all other deer nearby that danger lurks. When suddenly startled, this sound is singular and explosive; when deer have detected trouble from a distance, warning is often given in a series of lengthier snorts.

EYE SEE YOU

White-tailed deer's eyes are adapted to see well both in low light (even in darkness) as well as under the bright light of day. Their pupils contract into a narrow slit, unlike ours which form a circular opening. This slit concentrates light in a narrow band against the back of the eye, or retina, which contains the light sensing receptors clustered in a horizontal band. Scientists speculate that it is this horizontal arrangement that allow deer to see very well in a linear pattern, enhancing the ability to see across a wide area. Combined with the actual placement in the skull of the whitetail's eyes, they have a remarkable 270 degree field of view. The only place they can't see is behind them. Our field of view is limited to 180 degrees.

Whitetails can see better than we can in the dark.

Inside their eye, whitetails (and other animals designed to see in low light) have a membrane that you and I lack—the *tepetum lucidum.* It is this membrane that reflects the light of your car's headlights. It also allows light to reflect through their eye's light receptors twice, increasing their ability to see in the dark.

Why Are Fawns Spotted?

The most beautiful adaptation of the whitetail's coat is that of the fawn. Reddish brown in color, the fawn's coat also has two rows of white spots down either side of the spine, and an array of random white spots elsewhere. The effect of this, seen while the fawn is lying motionless in hiding, is that of the dappled effect of sunlight on the forest floor through the leaves of trees. Despite the fact that the spots are white, this dappled effect combined with the brown background makes fawns virtually invisible even from a few feet away.

The spots on a fawn's back are designed to mimic the dappled effect of sunlight on the forest floor.

TWO COATS IN ONE

Each year, deer grow and shed two coats. One for the summer, and one for winter. The winter coat is very specialized. Comprised partially of darker, sun-absorbing guard hairs, it sports a second layer of woolly underfur. There are five times as many of these crinkled under-hairs as there are the longer guard hairs. Like a sheep's wool, or your down-filled parka, this dense underfur creates numerous pockets of dead-air that trap body heat, providing excellent insulation. Unlike their summer coat, the winter coat's individual guard hairs are hollow, further increasing the amount of dead air space and insulation. So little heat escapes that snow falling on a deer doesn't melt. In fact, deer sometimes allow themselves to be covered by falling snow, since the snow also provides a layer of insulation. Whitetails can also increase their coat's insulation effectiveness by "puffing" up their hair. This is an involuntary reaction to frigid temperatures made possible by a specialized muscle at the root of the hair called "arrector pili." When erected to their full height, the insulating layer of the hair is thickened. (You and I, by the way, have the same specialized muscles. But since we no longer have much body hair, the end result are "goose bumps" —not exactly a great aid in keeping warm.)

Their summer coat is much smoother and reddish in color. There are fewer hairs in the summer coat than in the winter version, and because these hairs lack the pigment melanin that gives the winter coat its blackish tones, this reddish summer coat reflects sunlight to help keep them cool.

Why Such Bright White Tails?

Considering whitetails have evolved a coat that keeps them protected from the elements and is designed to "protect" them from predators through camouflage, one might wonder why they have such a conspicuous white tail.

This "flag" serves an important purpose. Many grassland ungulates evolved a white rump patch that serves as a beacon to others of their kind in order to form herd cohesiveness. One

might easily argue that the white rump is also easier for young or trailing members to follow in a dusty stampede away from predators. White-tailed deer, however, aren't herd animals, or creature of the open. Their survival depends largely on being unseen in the forest. Nonetheless, they are social animals that need to keep track of each other. Thus they evolved a tail that meets both needs— when up, it is a flag that signals a warning or that others can follow; when down, it is brown, completing their camouflage!

ANTLERS

Antlers are the male deer's way of saying "I'm big and healthy" to the females in the hope that they will mate, and "I'm big, don't mess with me" to rival males.

People are fascinated by deer with large antlers. Why? I have my own theory. Since humans have been hunters for about as long as we've been human, I think the appreciation for large antlers is hard wired into our genetic code. Sure, we appreciate the beauty and symmetry of these antlers, but really, I think we like them for a very practical ancestral reason.

Today, there is a saying among hunters that "you can't eat antlers," meaning that it is just fine to shoot a small-antlered deer, or a doe. And it is. But to our ancestors, big deer simply meant more deer. In other words, if you have a choice between an antler-less or small-racked deer and a behemoth with a large rack—and your winter survival depends on the quantity of meat you collect—you would always choose the big-racked animal. Antlers for our ancestors quickly conveyed which of the animals would offer up the most meat.

Bucks produce their first antlers in the spring just prior to their first birthday, although fawn bucks sometimes grow short buttons (not to be confused with the longer "spikes" of some yearling bucks). Antler growth is triggered by the pineal gland, which in turns triggers the release of testosterone, the hormone most responsible for antler growth. The pineal gland is sensitive to photoperiod; antler growth begins as the days lengthen in spring, between the spring equinox and summer solstice. Whitetails in the far north have a more defined schedule to their antler growth than those near the equator. Minnesota bucks are growing antlers by May, while those in Florida won't start until June.

Antler growth is incredibly rapid and is, in fact, the fastest growing bone known. Although antler growth is started by the lengthening of days in spring, it is hastened by the shortening days of late summer. By the time the rut occurs, most buck's antlers will have been hardened bone for two full months.

Velvet

Growing antlers are covered in a modified skin and fur known as velvet. Rich with blood and nerve tissues, velvet nourishes the growing bone, and consists almost completely of a protein called collagen. Antlers are susceptible to damage when in velvet, and an injured antler bleeds profusely, but clots quickly. Misshapen antlers are often a result of accidental damage during this growth period.

Antler growth begins from the pedicles, which are specialized parts of the forehead. Stimulated by the hormone testosterone, antlers are actually living bone, in which blood is supplied via a complex network of tiny capillaries. In late summer/early autumn, the antler bone mineralizes and hardens, halting the blood flow.

DEER ANTLER VELVET— AN APHRODISIAC?

A 2,000-year-old scroll discovered in a tomb in Hunan Province, China, lists dozens of different diseases that could be treated with velvet deer antler. The 16th century "Materia Medica," a standard text of Chinese herbalists, lists deer antler velvet as one of the most highly prized natural medicinal substances.

Deer antler velvet contains many substances including amino acids, minerals, proteins, anti-inflammatory peptides, and hormones thought by some, especially Asians, to increase sexual performance and desire. It is still sold worldwide, and is harvested from live, captive deer before the velvet dies and hardens. There is no scientific evidence, though, that it really works!

The velvet dies over a twenty-four hour period, and bucks thrash it from their new hard, white antlers. During this process, bloody surfaces are exposed, and the blood, in combination with the juices of the plants and trees the buck is now thrashing, stains the antlers in shades from mahogany to coffee.

HOW ARE ANTLERS DIFFERENT THAN HORNS?

The antlers that grow on male mule deer, elk, and moose are made of solid bone. While the antlers are growing, they are soft and tender and covered with a thin skin, called velvet, which contains thousands of blood vessels. Late in the winter, antlers are shed, and the growing process starts again. Horns, in contrast, are never shed. Horns have no blood supply and are made of keratin—a hard protein that is the same as your fingernails.

So What Are Antlers For?

White-tailed deer antlers sweep forward on the main beam, then grow upward on the tines. This basket shape seems to be designed to "catch" the antlers of an equal size opponent, thus lowering the risk of injury to either combatant. Antler size is determined by both nutrition and genetics. That is, some deer just have the genes for big antlers, but even then, their antlers won't be as big as they could be without good nutrition. With both good nutrition and the right genes, a yearling buck (his second fall) may have three or four points per side. Lacking one or the other of these elements, his first rack may only consist of two single spikes.

Antlers do serve the whitetail buck as weapons against predators and other whitetail rivals. But, for the most part, these elaborate ornaments are there so bucks *won't* have to fight, at least among themselves. Social dominance in the male whitetail's world is largely governed by size of body and size of antlers. Since large bucks generally also produce large antlers, this head gear serves as a visual means of displaying one's status. Small bucks fear large bucks, limiting the rare actual combat to rivals of equal stature. Thus ,in the grand evolutionary mastery of nature, these fascinating antlers, though they could be used for deadly means, prevent most fights simply through display.

Antlers are cast in January through March, again as a reaction to photoperiod. At the point where the antler erupts from the skull is a joint known as the pedicle. Resulting from decreased testosterone after the rut, the bond between antler and pedicle weakens, and the two antlers fall off, often within hours of each other.

MAKING BABIES

Among large mammals, white-tailed deer are considered a prolific species. They reach puberty at an early age (as fawns in some populations, as yearlings in all others). Exactly when they reach puberty has much to do with the quality of their range, since the onset of puberty is determined by body weight. With good habitat and a low enough population density, fawns can reach the weight needed—70 pounds for southern deer; 80 pounds for those in the north—by their first autumn. In general, though, it is best for a population if fawns don't breed.

24 Hours to Mate

White-tailed deer does are only in estrus for about 24 hours, and must find a mate during that short window of opportunity. Until that time, she will not breed with a buck. However, nature has provided a back-up plan. If she goes un-mated during her first estrus, she'll experience another estrus one month later. Bucks wander widely during the rut so that they have a greater chance of encountering does who are in estrus.

Does Rule! Does choose the buck they mate with, not the other way around. If she doesn't want to mate with an inferior buck, she'll drive him off with her front hooves.

Whereas most bucks don't reach their physical peak until they are five years old (in some heavily hunted areas, "old" bucks may merely be three and a half years old; in more pristine settings, some bucks retain dominance status past ten years of age), does are sexually active by the time they are yearlings. A doe's breeding success improves with age until she is about eight years old. Once mature, she'll usually bear twins, and is a skillful mother. Given this scenario, a doe may have as many as eight or nine fawns before a same-age buck mates for the first time.

YOUNG PARENTS

Fawn does and bucks don't typically breed, but in some populations and situations they do. Fawn does that breed lack the birthing and rearing skills of older does, tend to breed later in the season (which results in later birthing dates that leave their fawns little time to grow before winter), and have a higher rate of still-births and fawn abandonment. Fawn bucks (and yearlings) that breed have not been tested by the rigors of life. Usually, nature insures that young bucks don't breed, but in populations where too many mature bucks have been removed, young bucks do get a chance to reproduce.

It's clear, then, that how quickly a deer population grows depends on the number of does. In mathematical terms, does "multiply" while bucks "add" or "subtract." Does, of course, "multiply" themselves. Remove a doe from a population and you remove not just one deer, but at least two or three (the doe, and the one or two fawns she would have born the next spring), and perhaps even more if you consider that she might have lived to reproduce for a number of years. Remove a buck from the population and you merely subtract one deer. Because of the early age at which does breed, and the number of fawns they can carry, white-tailed deer in good habitat can double their population in just two years.

Since whitetails have a 200 day gestation period, most mating north of 40 degrees latitude occurs during the cool, short days of late October and early November, just before the first serious snowfalls. Although the rut will not cease if an early storm hits the north woods, deep snow can make it difficult for bucks to travel as widely as needed to service all of the does. Move a little further south to between 36 and 40 degrees latitude, as well as in most southeastern states, and the rut happens in November and December. South of 36 degrees latitude, especially in the American southwest and into Mexico, the rut happens in January and February. White-tailed deer in Central and South America breed year-round.

FAWN FACTS

• Does give birth either while standing or lying down, and the exact spot seems chosen haphazardly.

• Twins, which are the norm with experienced mothers, are born about fifteen minutes apart.

• Triplets are not unusual with prime-age does, but fawn and yearling does usually give birth to a single fawn.

• A normal, healthy fawn weighs about six to nine pounds.

• Immediately after giving birth, the doe carefully and thoroughly licks her fawns clean. She also consumes the afterbirth and all the fluid-stained vegetation to minimize odors that might lure predators.

• Whitetails produce a very rich milk that, for a short time after birth, is also laden with necessary antibodies.

• Fawns nurse within moments of birth, and within twenty minutes of being born, they are able to walk.

IN A RUT

We consider being in a rut a bad thing, but it ain't so for deer. The rut is the climax of their year, both for does and bucks, because it is the mating season, and their chance to pass on their genes. It's what they survived for all the rest of the year.

The rut, which is brought about by hormonal changes triggered by the changing length of daylight, brings on lots of behavioral changes. As the rut intensifies, does go through some conflicting urges. They become less protective of this year's fawns, and so will allow yearlings of the previous year to rejoin them, forming larger, family units. However, does will not allow the return of their yearling buck offspring. If a yearling buck tried to return to his mother, she will drive him away to avoid his breeding with her or any other of his near relatives.

As she succumbs to the inevitable urges of hormones, a doe becomes increasingly restless, often at night. Within her home range is a section that she considers her "core" area. Some evidence indicates that, despite her restlessness, she confines her movements to this core. Like the buck who wanders and advertises his presence through rubs and scrapes, the intense use of this core area may make it easier for the buck to find her. As she continues to bed and urinate in this area, her scent permeates it. The sensitive nose of the whitetail buck must be able to detect this amorous doe's boudoir.

(Below left) a buck rubs his antlers on a pine tree; (below right) a buck scrape; (opposite left) making a rub; (opposite right) incisor scrapings on a hemlock tree.

Whitetail bucks aren't truly territorial. They will tolerate the presence of other breeding age bucks as long as these other bucks retain subordinate behavior. This probably works as much to the subordinate buck's advantage as it does to the dominant buck. By being able to "hang around," a subordinate buck can potentially find a mate during the dominant buck's absence since within a dominant buck's range, more than one doe may come into estrus at the same time. Even dominant bucks can't tend to two does in two locations at the same time.

Sparring Matches

Sparring matches between bucks are different than dominance fights. Sparring usually represents low-level aggression, and often occurs even before the rut begins. It seems to be a way for bucks to test each other without the risk of full battle, which can lead to injury. Often, after a brief sparring match, bucks will resume feeding side by side, as if nothing had ever occurred.

Dominance fights between rival bucks rarely lead to death, but that outcome does occur. Sometimes the combatants' antlers become locked, leading to the death of one or both. Bucks have been seen with the entire head and rack of a rival still locked in theirs, apparently able to paw themselves free of the rival's dead body with their sharp hooves. Injuries, such as puncture wounds or eye loss, also, yet both death and injury are fairly rare. The whitetail's rack, with its basket shape, is designed to "catch" an opponent, not spear him, lowering the risk of serious injury or death. In addition, most dominance fights are short lived—less than a minute. In that brief time, though, an incredible amount of energetic shoving and twisting is involved, and bucks seem to be able to quickly assess their rival's abilities. It is better for the "loser" to break off the fight and flee so that he might breed elsewhere than to risk death or injury battling a superior rival.

"I think I'm getting buck fever."

BUCK SCRAPES— MESSAGES WRITTEN IN DIRT

Buck scrapes are an important form of whitetail communication. They let other bucks know who's boss of the neighborhood, and they also serve to let does know that a breeding age buck will again be passing this way. Scrapes are a message—a note made of odors—and the dominant buck's way of asserting himself even when he can't physically be present. Bucks urinate into the middle of the scrape, hunching slightly, down the inside of his rear legs while rubbing his tarsal glands together. The message tells other bucks to stay away, and tells does that a suitable mate is nearby. Does will sometimes urinate in the buck scrape to let him know that she's ready to breed.

(Opposite left) an antler rub on a large tree with a scrape beneath; (opposite right) a buck scrape; (above) a buck has grass hanging from his antlers after raking in the grass during the rut.

DEER YARDS

No, a deer yard isn't a place where whitetails have cook-outs. In the northern portion of the whitetail's range, deer yards are important winter survival areas. These places are characterized by dense stands of cedars or other conifers, which tend to deflect snow and also provide protection from wind, thus minimizing heat loss. Deer gather in these areas during the long winter months.

Eventually, the rut ceases. But like its beginning, it doesn't happen abruptly. Decreasing daylight again causes photoreceptive responses in both bucks and does, slowing the mating urge. Those does not bred during the first cycle will come into estrus about a month later. Bucks with enough testosterone still coursing through their veins will find and mate with them. But gradually, and surely, the rush to reproduce ends. Deer travel to winter habitats to pass the winter. Does concentrate on preserving their strength so that it might go to nourish the embryos they carry. Bucks seek a rest to regain their lost vigor, and by January, will drop the impressive racks that they had grown at such an expense. Winter is a time for subsistence, but the seeds have been planted, and spring awaits.

"I've always wondered how they kept track of all their rubs and scrapes."

DEER IN WINTER

Whitetails in the north shift from their home range to their winter range in response to sharp drops in temperature. In order to deal with cold temperatures and to make their stored reserves last longer, whitetails have the ability to lower their metabolic rate. This lower rate kicks in when temperatures drop below 45 degrees F, and is in full swing once the mating season is over. It remains at low ebb until the lengthening days of March. Throughout the winter, whitetails are less active and voluntarily reduce their food intake. By the end of the winter they may lose over twenty percent of their body weight as they subsist on their body fat. If hard pressed, whitetails are able to survive for over a month without eating.

WINTER'S WRATH

Biologists in northern states have developed indices to judge how many deer will die due to winter weather. In Minnesota, for instance, a Winter Severity Index assigns one point for each day the temperature is below zero degrees F, and another point for each day the snow depth is fifteen inches or more. A moderate winter in the northern section of this state falls somewhere between 100 and 150 points. Using this formula, biologists predict that at 100 points, 5 percent of the adult deer and 10 percent of fawns will die over the course of a winter. At 150 points, those statistics rise to 21 and 29 percent respectively. A severe winter in which 175 points accumulate will result in 28 percent of adults and 38 percent of fawns dying due to starvation. When such die-offs occur, wildlife managers reduce the number of antlerless deer licenses made available to hunters, allowing whitetail numbers to rebuild, often in as short a period as two years.

Deer gather in deer yards during the long winter months.

SOCIAL ORDER

It may seem contradictory to say that the white-tailed deer is both a secretive loner, and a social animal, but both descriptions fit, largely depending on the time of the year. Although whitetails do gather at times, rarely do these gatherings take on the behavior of a herd. Most large scale gatherings are relatively short lived, unlike the full-time herd lifestyle of bison, and should the deer become alarmed, they don't bolt off in a herd-like stampede. Instead, it's every deer for itself. Still, whitetails don't live by themselves all the time. They know and interact with all the other deer in their range, and in so doing, they act in a socially predictable manner.

"I figure they'll hole up in a warm, cozy place till this storm is over."

Adult deer segregate by sex much of the year, beginning with the fawning season. Nonbreeding yearling does, sometimes joined by yearling bucks, gather in groups for the summer, and often rejoin their mother come early autumn. Fraternal, or bachelor groups, form during the fawning season as well, and remain together through the summer and into early fall. Yearling bucks, freshly driven from their mothers, seek the company of each other and older, dominant males. Fraternal groups can be quite small—perhaps only a pair of compatible bucks—when deer densities are low or hunting pressure has removed many bucks. They tend to be larger in open country, regardless of deer densities. Members of bachelor groups, unlike those in the doe groups, usually aren't related.

Deer & People

In an ever more crowded world, deer and
people are destined to share the same space.
After all, we are two of the most adaptable species
on the planet! This sometimes leads to conflicts, but
it also leads to pleasures. People enjoy watching deer, and
some feed them in their backyards to increase that pleasure.
Others enjoy hunting them, and eating them too!

The problems of too many deer can be significant. Crop damage to farms, damage to landscaping, and vehicle-deer collisions cost money, and even lives. White-tailed deer are also known to be a vector for transmitting Lyme's disease.

Over the three hundred years between the arrival of Columbus and the colonization of the United States from coast to coast, whitetail numbers fluctuated repeatedly. Indian and white hunters killed large numbers for meat and hides to send to market. Settlers often depended heavily on native game while they scratched clear the ancient forest to make room for

"Deer hunting means a lot to this little town."

their farms. When these farms failed, as they often did, and the settlers moved even further west, depleted deer populations rebounded temporarily as nature reclaimed the clearings, providing prime whitetail habitat. This cycle repeated itself many times in the settling of North America.

In the late 1800s, once the continent was laced with roads and railroads that could carry both settlers west and white-tailed deer parts to market, the real extermination of deer began. Venison was a popular staple of city dwellers and was found on the menu of many fine restaurants and for sale in markets. In order to feed this demand, market hunters took to the woods. At the same time, residents of burgeoning rural communities went afield to hunt whitetails. With no hunting seasons or bag limits, a growing human population took a heavy toll on not only white-tailed deer, but many other native species. Although this era's unregulated sport hunting contributed to the whitetail's decline, the larger blame can be laid on an insatiable appetite for venison in the cities and a desire for the supple leather created from the deer's hide.

POPULARITY OF DEER

Deer are important to both hunters and non-hunters. Various studies across the country have found that among non-hunters, deer are the most popular type of wildlife. (Source: Wisconsin DNR)

In the United States there are 115 towns, cities, townships, and counties named Deer; 14 named Moose; four named Caribou; and 96 named Elk, Elkhorn, or similar (Source: U.S. Census Bureau)

The pressure on white-tailed deer only diminished when they became so difficult to find that it was no longer profitable to go afield. In many areas of the country they were extinct, and in others only remnant populations remained. From a pre-Columbus population of somewhere between 23 and 33 million, the whitetail's numbers crashed to an estimated low of 350,000 - 500,000 thousand by 1900.

Early hunter-conservationists were instrumental in seeking laws to protect this highly esteemed and beautiful animal; the very root of wildlife management in this country started here. With the advent of controlled hunting seasons and bag limits, combined with the new science of wildlife management, white-tails climbed back from these low numbers.

While human intervention was essential to the restoration of whitetails throughout its range, their secretive ways and flexible nature insured that, given half a chance, they would respond in the same fruitful manner that they had for eons. And their evolutionary course, which adapted them to forest edges and a wide range of foods, proved invaluable as they spread back out into a world very much changed by the invasion of Europeans. Without this flexibility, white-tailed deer might yet be a rare species.

DEER HERD SIZE: PROBLEMS & PLEASURE

The deer herd size creates both opportunity and consequences for people. As densities approach 20 deer per square mile of deer habitat, the herd can browse enough trees to substantially reduce the yield of high-value trees. Pine plantations and Christmas tree operations are particularly hard hit by large herds. Orchardists and farmers also feel the pinch from a large herd. Damage to corn, soybeans, alfalfa, hay, vegetables, strawberries, and fruit orchards increases as the herd size grows. On the fringes of urban development, deer eat ornamental plantings and damage native plants.

This photo shows the browse line on wild grapes.

On the other hand, a large deer herd is a real pleasure for those who enjoy the challenge of hunting whitetails, eating venison, making fine sausages, sharing the camaraderie of a deer hunt, feeding deer, or just watching white-tailed deer throughout the seasons.

Fully two-thirds of the people who like to watch wild animals choose white-tailed deer as their favorite animal to see in the wild. In just Wisconsin alone, more than two million residents are wildlife watchers and they spend about $500 million on their hobby.

Again in Wisconsin, deer hunters annually buy $500 million worth of goods and services. These purchases generate $30 million in sales taxes and income taxes in that state. More than 8,000 people make a living from jobs directly related to deer hunting. License fees contribute $16 million each year to conservation programs carried out by the Wisconsin Department of Natural Resources. The hunting public also funds the majority of the Wildlife Damage Program that reimburses farmers for deer damage to crops.

"Your Realtree shirt clashes with your Mossy Oak pants."

DEER MANAGEMENT

Suppose your family owns 120 acres of land and they've appointed you the overseer. Each of them, from your brother-in-law the logger, to your wife the gardener, comes to you with their ideas on how the land should be managed.

Your brother-in-law wants a maximum yield of timber, especially for those species the mills want. Your wife prefers more open space, with fewer animals, like deer, that eat crops. Your father wants more old forest to benefit some of the birds he likes. Finally, your brother wants as many whitetails as the habitat can support. This scenario should give you the idea of just how complex deer management is for natural resource agencies who must consider all of these legitimate interests!

It used to be that wildlife managers had only season length and bag limits as whitetail management tools. In the "good old days," an unlimited number of deer licenses were available. Nature took its course, along with timber production, development, and agriculture, to randomly produce a deer herd. Either sex seasons were the norm until the 1970s in most states, and population monitoring was done by counting deer droppings.

LARGE SCALE FEEDING CAN'T SAVE WINTER DEER

Large scale feeding operations have proven to be a waste of time and money. Succumbing to political pressure, the Minnesota Department of Natural Resources launched a massive feeding effort during the severe winter of 1988-1989. Over a million dollars was spent to deliver four thousand tons of pellets to forest whitetails in a 46,000 square mile area in the northern region of the state. To do so, 17,000 hours of DNR time, and 230,000 hours of volunteer time was needed. The result? Because forest areas are virtually impenetrable in the winter, workers could only get food to 10 percent of the deer, and only three percent more deer survived than if no feeding had occurred. Better success can be had in agricultural regions, though, where whitetails are easier to reach in the smaller woodlots, and farm country's maze of roads makes delivering the food possible. (Source: Minnesota Department of Natural Resources)

Today's state wildlife managers have crafted whitetail programs that manage for the long haul, producing more deer and improved hunter success rates. But they also need to balance that with the needs of those who don't want deer eating their crops or shrubs, as well as manage populations to avoid car-deer collisions.

Instead of just bag and season limits, today's wildlife managers have real management tools that fall into five categories: population monitoring; deer research; coordinating deer habitat needs into timber sales; public land habitat improvement; and private land habitat improvement.

Research proves that the best way to control deer numbers is to regulate doe harvest. Wildlife managers issue fewer antlerless tags in zones where deer increases are desirable and, where numbers are high, issue more "doe" tags to help bring the population in balance with the habitat.

Hunters may think of researchers as geeks in lab frocks, but such isn't the case for researchers who spend long hours in the woods. If you want to know how many deer the land can support, while recognizing the reality of increased development and timber production, you need to know just what age forest, what tree species, and the proper mix of both that are necessary for deer survival.

Deer & Vehicles

White-tailed deer are responsible for about 150 human deaths each year in more than 1.5 million traffic accidents involving collisions with deer, according to an insurance industry-funded report that puts the economic damage at $1.1 billion. It is estimated that each year in the United States, 29,000 people are also injured in such collisions. About two-thirds of deer-vehicle accidents occur during October, November, and December, especially in the early morning and at dusk, because deer are most active during the months in which they breed. More human injuries occur when drivers swerve to avoid deer and collide with roadside obstacles or vehicles in the opposing lane than if they hit the animal. The average insurance claim for a deer-car collision is $2,000.

More than 1.5 million traffic accidents involve collisions with deer each year.

DEER COSTS

Annual estimates of deer damage are reported to exceed $2 billion nationwide, including $1 billion in car damages, more than $100 million in agricultural crop damage, $750 million in damage to the timber industry, and more than $250 million in damage to metropolitan households (e.g., landscape plantings). These estimates are conservative, and it is often difficult to obtain reliable statistics for wildlife-related losses.

Deer frequently feed on flowers, fruits, and vegetables and the buds and twigs of fruit trees and ornamental shrubs. Damage to landscape plantings and ornamentals may occur at any time of year but is usually most severe in the late winter and early spring when other food supplies are limited. Damage to fruit trees may cause both the immediate loss of the crop and residual tree injury that leads to reduced yields in the future. Deer browsing may permanently disfigure ornamental trees.

BUZZ OFF, DEER!

Repellents can help prevent deer from feeding on crops or landscaping plants. Repellents fall into two broad categories—those that repel by taste and those that repel with a disagreeable odor. Hinder, an ammonium soap-based repellent, and Deer-Off, a product that incorporates putrescent egg solids, are two repellents currently approved for use on garden vegetables and fruit-bearing trees during the growing season.
Source: Cornell University

HOW DEER AFFECT OTHER PLANTS & ANIMALS

Like people, deer affect their environment. Whitetails are big herbivores that eat large quantities of a wide variety of plants, thus impacting the abundance of these plants and the other animals that depend on these same plants for their habitat. This push-and-pull is only natural, but when do the number of deer have too great an effect on the environment? This question becomes a judgment call, and the following summarizes key research findings:

- Some leafy plants are stressed when deer populations swell to more than 12-15 animals per square mile. The foliage gets nipped back, which cuts into the plants' energy reserves, reducing successful reproduction. Plants like the bluebead lily and trillium are prime targets for deer.

- Trees and shrubs, particularly cedar, oak and Canada yew, are favored deer foods. When deer populations rise above 20-25 animals per square mile, these trees are heavily browsed and have a tough time surviving.

- Deer don't normally eat invertebrates, but insects that rely on certain plants may be harmed if the deer graze on their host species.

- It is likewise unlikely that deer directly harm reptiles and amphibians, but deer may harm their habitat. For instance, the western glass lizard relies on the same shrubs for shade in summer that deer eat in abundance.

- There is limited evidence that as deer numbers rise above 25 per square mile, habitat for small mammals is destroyed. The red-backed vole, for instance, needs a dense understory of low plants to survive.

- Deer numbers greater than 15-30 per square mile can browse back the shrubs and leafy plants some birds favor for food and cover. Populations of the black-throated blue warbler and the more rare hooded warbler can be affected by deer-browsed habitat.

- It is unlikely that moose populations would be restored anywhere we maintain a large deer herd. Deer carry a brainworm that causes a lethal meningitis-like illness in moose. Elk, on the other hand, are not threatened by the meningeal brainworm, nor do elk compete with deer for the same foods.

Is the deer herd self-limiting? Yes, but wildlife managers work to keep the herd below that density. As the herd approaches the habitat's carrying capacity, deer mortality increases, reproductive rates drop, and the herd gets weaker and less healthy. (Source: Wisconsin Dept. of Natural Resources).

LYME DISEASE

There is also a public health concern regarding white-tailed deer because they are one of the hosts for the ticks responsible for the spread of Lyme disease, an arthritic disease that can be contracted by humans.

According to the Centers for Disease Control, there were more than 16,000 cases of Lyme disease nationwide in 1998, up from approximately 2,000 cases in 1987. New York State had 3,325 cases of Lyme disease in 1997, the highest number of

reported cases in the United States, followed by Connecticut, Pennsylvania, and New Jersey. Lyme disease has reached epidemic proportions on Long Island and in portions of the lower Hudson Valley.

Deer serve as one of several potential hosts for the black-legged tick (*Ixodes scapularis*), which transmits the bacterial spirochete *Borrelia burgdorferi* that causes Lyme disease. Larval and nymphal ticks commonly feed on whitefooted mice and other mammals and birds. Adult ticks prefer deer as their host, although they may also occur on medium-sized mammals such as raccoons and opossum. Tick abundance has been found to be positively correlated with deer density.

CHRONIC WASTING DISEASE

Chronic Wasting Disease (CWD) is a contagious neurological disease affecting deer and elk. It causes a characteristic spongy degeneration of the brains of infected animals resulting in emaciation, abnormal behavior, loss of bodily functions, and death.

CWD belongs to a group of diseases known as transmissible spongiform encephalopathies (TSEs). Within this family of diseases, there are several other variants that affect domestic animals: scrapie, which has been identified in domestic sheep and goats for more than 200 years; bovine spongiform encephalopathy (BSE) in cattle (also known as "mad cow disease"); and transmissible mink encephalopathy in farmed mink. Only three species of the deer family are known to be naturally susceptible to CWD: elk, mule deer, and white-tailed deer.

The origin of CWD is unknown, and it may never be possible to definitively determine how or when CWD arose. It was first recognized as a syndrome in captive mule deer held in wildlife research facilities in Colorado in the late 1960s, but it was not identified as a TSE until the 1970s. Computer modeling suggests the disease may have been present in free-ranging populations of mule deer for more than 40 years.

WHERE IS CWD FOUND?

Chronic Wasting Disease was long thought to be limited in the wild to a relatively small endemic area in northeastern Colorado, southeastern Wyoming, and southwestern Nebraska, but it has recently been found in new areas of these states, as well as in wild deer and elk in western South Dakota, and wild deer in northern Illinois, south-central New Mexico, northeastern Utah, south-central Wisconsin, central New York, and west-central Saskatchewan. The disease also has been diagnosed in commercial game farms in Colorado, Nebraska, Minnesota, South Dakota, Montana, Oklahoma, Kansas, Wisconsin, Saskatchewan, and Alberta. In a report released by the University of Saskatchewan, the expert panel concluded that CWD "is arguably the most important issue in the management of free-living cervids in North America. The disease has the potential to reduce cervid populations in the long-term, and to create major socio-economic impacts as observed in other areas in North America" and that CWD was likely introduced to wild deer as a result of "spill-over from infected game farms."

Deer Hunting

Many people today have a tendency to view our ancestors, especially those ancient ancestors who practiced a hunter-gatherer lifestyle, as primitive, and therefore somehow less intelligent. The view that a hunter-gathering lifestyle is primitive (in the pejorative sense) derives from the conscious efforts of social scientists who, through the 1960s and into the 1990s, sought to discredit this lifestyle, seeing the drawing of blood as somehow politically incorrect. Depicted by these revisionist sociologists as perpetually impoverished, hunter-gatherers were portrayed as people barely able to sustain themselves, and therefore incapable of the loftier thoughts we attribute to agrarian and industrial societies.

Hunting submerges man deliberately in that formidable mystery and therefore contains something of a religious rite and emotion in which homage is paid to what is divine, transcendent, in the laws of nature.

—Jose Ortega y Gassett

In fact, the hunter-gatherer lifestyle is the oldest, most successful way of human life, and worldwide, is responsible for some of the most elaborate and beautiful mythologies and theologies ever developed.

Until quite recently, in geologic terms, all humans were hunter-gatherers. Pre-human hominids (our ancestors) may have adopted a hunter-gatherer lifestyle as long ago as three million years. As a species, our ability to spread across the globe was largely made possible by our ability to find suitable food, especially meat, no matter where we ventured. Most anthropologists agree that humans were fully modern—physically and intellectually our equals—at least one hundred thousand years ago. For most of the time since then, we've been hunter-gatherers. Even once we developed agriculture—only ten thousand years ago, and even then in only some parts of the world—at least a part of our time was still spent in hunting and foraging wild crops.

...and when some of my friends have asked me anxiously about their boys, whether they should let them hunt, I have answered, yes—remembering that it was one of the best parts of my education—make them hunters, though sportsmen only at first, if possible mighty hunters at last, so that they shall not find game large enough for them in this or any other vegetable wilderness— hunters as well as fishers of men.

—Henry David Thoreau

While some view deer hunting in a negative light, most deer hunters care deeply about the environment. Hunters also donate a lot of venison to food pantries; from 1997-2004, deer hunters donated 1,600 tons of venison to those in need, which equals 12,800,000 meals. (Source: Farmers and Hunters Feeding the Hungry)

Although there are places left in the world where hunting is still a physical necessity, most hunting today takes place because we want to, not because we need to. Today's hunters pursue deer for a variety of reasons: meat, excitement, time out-of-doors, and to be with family and friends.

Deer hunting is unquestionably the most popular form of hunting in the United States. According to the National Survey of Fishing, Hunting, and Wildlife-Associated Recreation performed by the U.S. Fish and Wildlife Service, there were 10.3 million deer hunters in 2001. For individuals over 16 years of age, nearly 1 in every 20 Americans and 8 in 10 hunters hunted deer in 2001, and their hunting-related expenditures while seeking deer totaled nearly $10.7 billion.

Deer is clearly the species of choice for the majority of hunters in the U.S. The survey indicates that 79 percent, or 10.3 million of the 13 million hunters in the U.S., hunted for deer. Turkey is the second-most hunted species at 2.5 million. Behind turkey hunting, squirrel and rabbit follow at around 2 million each, and then several bird species at 1 to 1.5 million. About 4.3 million hunters, or 42 percent of all hunters, hunt deer and nothing else.

Deer As Food

The term "venison" originally referred to the edible flesh of any wild animal. During the Middle Ages in England, it referred to the flesh of any animal killed in the hunt. Wild boars, rabbits, hares, bears, etc. were all referred to as venison. Today, the term is used to refer to deer meat.

Venison is a very good source of protein, while, unlike most meats, it tends to be fairly low in fat, especially saturated fat. Four ounces of venison supplies 68.5 percent of the daily value for protein with only 179 calories and 1.4 grams of saturated fat. Venison is also a good source of iron, providing 28.2 percent of the daily value of iron in that same four-ounce serving. Venison is also a good source of vitamin B12 and several other of the B vitamins, including riboflavin, niacin, and vitamin B6.

Venison—How does it stack up?

Meat (3 oz)	Calories	Fat (grams)	Saturated Fat	Cholesterol (milligrams)
Deer	128	2 g	1 g	67 mg
Elk	134	2 g	1 g	62 mg
Moose	114	1 g	1 g	66 mg
Beef tenderloin	185	9 g	4 g	71 mg
Pork tenderloin	159	5 g	2 g	80 mg

(Source: U.S. Department of Agriculture Nutrient Data Laboratory, 2004)

Venison or Veganism?

Which food source costs the planet less is kilocalories of fossil fuel energy—venison or vegetables?

Calculations made for his book **BLOOD TIES** by environmental writer Ted Kerasote, and by Dr. David Pimentel of Cornell University, show venison costs the planet less. Pimentel helped Kerasote compare 150 pounds of elk meat with equal food calories of potatoes, rice, and beans:

• VENISON: 79,000 kilocalories of fossil fuel (includes costs of producing vehicle, fuel, gun, ammo, and electricity for freezer)

• POTATOES from region: 151,000 kilocalories (farm machinery, transportation of food, planting/harvesting)

• California grown RICE & BEANS: 477,000 kilocalories (farm machinery, transportation, planting/harvesting)

A peculiar virtue in wildlife ethics is that the hunter ordinarily has no gallery to applaud or disapprove of his conduct. Whatever his acts, they are dictated by his own conscience, rather than by a mob of onlookers.

—Aldo Leopold

Historians think that venison has been consumed as a food longer than other meats, including beef, chicken, and pork. While venison and other wild game have roamed the lands for millennia, the practice of domesticating venison for food seems to have begun in ancient times, during the Stone Age. While the ancient Greeks printed a guide to hunting, the ancient Romans lauded the pleasures of hunting and consuming wild game.

Today, venison is enjoyed by many cultures that still rely on hunting for their food. In addition, farm-raised venison is becoming more popular. New Zealand and the United States are the leading countries specializing in the domestication of venison today.

DEER TAILS & TRAILS 117

PHOTO CREDITS